LET AUGMENTED REALITY CHANGE HOW YOU READ A BOOK

With your smartphone, iPad or tablet you can use the **Neighbur Vue** app to invoke the augmented reality experience to literally read outside the book.

neighbur

  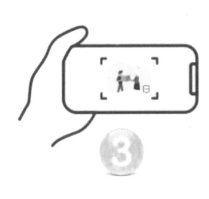

1. Notice the spelling: download the Neighbur Vue app from the Apple App Store or Google Play

(hint: searching for "Vue Neighbur" often works well)

2. Open and select the [vue] (vue) option

3. Point your lens at the full image with the [vue] and enjoy the augmented reality experience.

Go ahead and try it right now with the cover of this book.

Once the content begins, click the ⬆ (unlocked) 'Lock' icon to lock the content onto your phone.

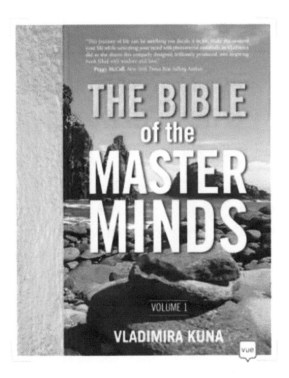

In praise of
The Bible of the Masterminds

"This journey of life can be anything you decide it to be. Make the most of your life while saturating your mind with phenomenal materials, as Vladimira did as she shares this uniquely designed, brilliantly produced, awe-inspiring book filled with wisdom and love. I love the design of this book and the message contained within. I am confident you will too."

—Peggy McColl,
***New York Times* Best-Selling Author**

"This compilation of easy-to-digest words of wisdom, coupled with true-life pictorial representations of Vladi's world adventures, will quickly become an essential part of your daily routine. When I first met Vladi, I was struck by her unquenchable thirst for growth and personal development. This book is a labour of love. It will leave you empowered and will make you grow."

—Gena West,
Award-winning Singer/Songwriter and Television Host
of *"A Different View with Gena West"*

"*The Bible of the Masterminds* is a fantastic asset for anyone serious about improving their lives. A collection of the ideas of some of the most intelligent and successful minds the world has ever seen, this book will serve as a constant reminder to stay the course to your wildest of dreams."

—Jamie Naegele
International Best-selling Author of *Who Are You?*
The Art of Being Yourself in a World Full of Masks

"Vladimira, you have creatively presented and shared your book with a daily dose of wisdom and love, connecting it to the splendours of nature. There is no downside to what you have done as you have proven that when you give, just give yourself."

—**David Grodski**
Retired Doctor and Author of
The Wisdom Of Wellness (WOW)

"Profound, beautiful and inspiring, Vladimira's book has captured the spirit of the inner work that precedes success and fulfillment in every walk of life. Steeped in wisdom, this is a book that you'll refer to again and again."

—**Annabelle Beckwith**
Business Consultant, Coach and Trainer
International Best-selling Author of *Get Your Peas In A Row:*
5 key factors to propel your business forward

"I have to say that I really enjoyed working on your book. I loved reading all the quotes. It made me feel so good inside to be constantly inspired (which is the purpose of the book). I think it's a very unique book idea and it was an absolute privilege to be part of the creative process."

—**Dave Falle**
Publishing & IT Director,
Hasmark Publishing International

As food is essential to the physical body, illumination and awareness is vital to our spiritual growth and development. Inspirational and picturesque, *The Bible of the Masterminds* is filled with heartfelt words of wisdom which stimulate purpose, faith and expectancy. Vladimira is a living example of how passion and persistence can transform a life and her personal testimony will inspire you to begin your journey of self-discovery and recognize the greatness within you.

—**Darryl Bell,**
Founder of Hope and Exchange,
International Best-selling Author of *We Are Creators*

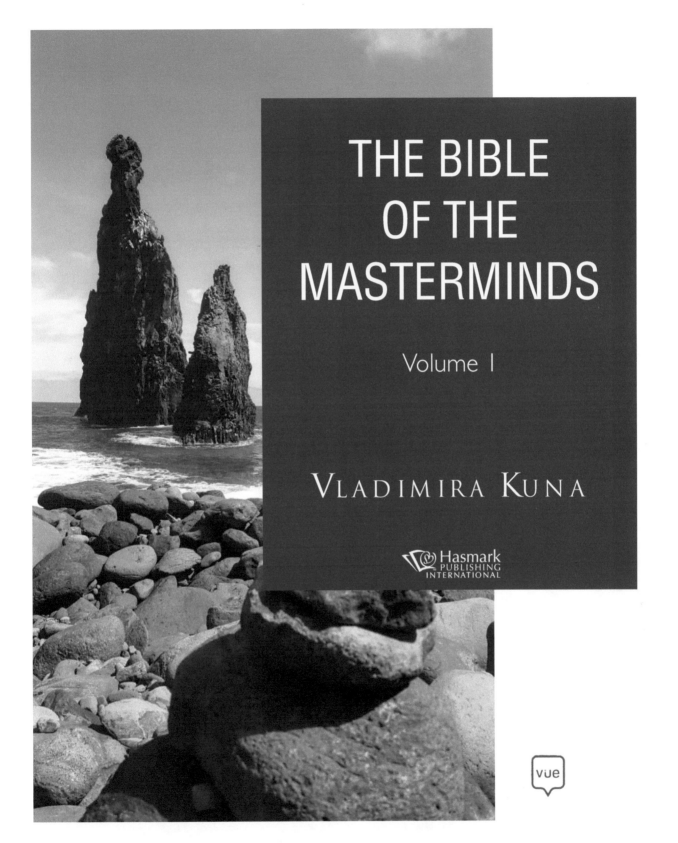

THE BIBLE
OF THE
MASTERMINDS

Volume I

VLADIMIRA KUNA

Hasmark
PUBLISHING
INTERNATIONAL

vue

Published by
Hasmark Publishing International
www.hasmarkpublishing.com

Permission should be addressed in writing to
Vladimira Kuna at admin@vladimirakuna.com at www.vladimirakuna.com

Editor: Gary Hoffman
gary.hoffman@live.com

Cover Design: Anne Karklins
anne@hasmarkpublishing.com

Book Design and Layout: Dave Falle
dave@hasmarkpublishing.com

Front cover photograph: Iain Forrest Photography

ISBN 13: 978-1-989756-51-5
ISBN 10: 1989756514

Dedication

To **Bob Proctor** and **Peggy McColl**,
my phenomenal mentors who helped
me to re-create myself.

I am so deeply and profoundly happy and grateful
to the Universe for connecting me to Bob
and his phenomenal teachings.

This book is a present for you, Bob.

Happy Birthday with love, gratitude and joy
from me and all the Master Minds who created
these inspiring quotes.

To **Joshua** and **Elizabeth**, my husband **Peter**,
and all my family and friends who
I love infinity x infinity.

Acknowledgments

I am so happy and grateful...

To **Bob Proctor**, the best of the best, whose phenomenal teaching is transforming the lives of millions around the world. May your legacy continue, forever influencing all of us. The enlightening idea to write this book came through studying Bob and Sandy's materials and I am forever grateful to the universe for connecting me with their teaching. It resonates with my one life substance. From the depths of heart, I am grateful for you. Thank you!

To **Joshua and Elizabeth**, my two most amazing creations filled with love, joy, full potential, everlasting open-minded power and strong will to achieve anything you desire...and to amazing, spiritual, and strong-minded Veronika. Love you infinity x infinity. Thank you!

To my **husband Peter**, who supported me throughout this illuminating inside out journey in many ways. For giving me space to grow, for your patience and for making me stronger by your actions, thank you!

To **Mum and Dad**, who gave me life and taught me how to be the best version of me. For showing me how to be grateful, kind, helpful, full of faith and confidence, how to have a good attitude always, and for giving me freedom to make decisions, grow and experience life. Love you forever. Thank you!

To my **sister Katarina & Stefan**, to my **brother Martin & Andrea** and my amazingly spirited and joyful nephew **Tobias**. You are my rocks, my deepest friendships; supporting and inspiring me every minute and enlightening my life always. I love the most amazing spiritual connection I have with my brother and sister, my best friends for life. Thank you!

To **Marisa Peer**, an amazing and inspiring lady, who has helped me to unblock my limitations with her unique rapid transformational hypnotherapy for abundance. You kept me going in times I wanted to give up, so I am forever grateful to you. Thank you!

*To **Mindvalley** for abundance and open-minded thinking with all the amazing and spiritual connections you provide to the world. Thank you!*

*To **Rhonda Byrne** and her Secret, for being my green traffic light and setting me off on my phenomenal journey. Rhonda has inspired the world and brought love and joy to my entire existence, and to others. Thank you!*

*To **Michael Beckwith and Lisa Nichols** for their teaching that connected the only life substance there is with my existence. You are inspiring beings. Thank you!*

*To **Dasenka and Jirik**, who stood next to me on my spiritual journey like guardian angels for years, sending me light and supporting me fully. I am grateful to have you in my life and for all the love and support received. Thank you!*

*To **Gena West**, a beautiful, inspiring, and pure soul, who has impacted the lives of many. You made me feel so special and unique, and you help people grow just by meeting and talking to them. You are a true example of perfection! Thank you!*

*And to **all my beautiful friends and special people**, who made me who I am today...stronger, powerful, vibrant, loving, caring, happier, confident, helpful and so much more...you helped me to create the life and vision I desire. Thank you to Serzi, Martin, Petr, Jana, Jaruska, Jarka, Mirusiatko, Evicka, teta Ala s rodinou, Clare, Rosie, Sara, Michelle, Lilly, Sarah, Caroline and Rosie & John. Thank you!*

*To **Peggy McColl and Trace** for spreading their angel's wings over me when I hit the moment of fighting my paradigm that was pulling me back. Applying Bob's teaching the best I could, I kept going with all I had, my burning desire, gratitude, persistence, discipline, faith, joy and the vision of achieving my goal. I manifested Peggy and Trace into my life and they have turned it upside down in the best possible way. They gave me the best gift I could ask for and put their trust and belief in me. I am eternally grateful. Thanks a million!*

*To **every single one of you** who crossed my path and influenced me with anything that has helped me to grow and to become who I am, thank you! Good and bad experiences formed me and made me stronger. Thank you!*

*And to **you**, the reader, from the deepest part of my heart, I hope this book will open your mind and illuminate your inside journey and help you to find your purpose...or lead you further with your existing one. Thank you!*

May this book bring you love, joy, inspiration, and enlightenment.
Design your life. Always go after what you want.
I intend this for you and for the world!

Preface

I was first introduced to Bob Proctor's teaching several years ago, while watching The Secret. I kept coming back to the movie, books, and some of the materials, but it was more "shelf help rather than self-help," as Lisa Nichols would say.

My idea for this book was born when I took a Paradigm Shift webinar with the Proctor Gallagher Institute in November 2019. I quit my job, as it was making me miserable, and I made a committed decision to enroll in the Secret Science to Getting Rich program, which I did in February 2020. And from that very moment, my life started to take the shape I desired.

The more I study the phenomenal materials and the more I understand the laws, the more I manifest incredible people and situations into my life. Just a simple understanding of the one substance expressing its directing power through us will guarantee you everything you want in your life.

Even today, Bob Proctor's voice still echoes in my mind. "What do you really want?" I can hear him repeating this sentence with that powerful, mind-absorbing voice. "What do you really want?" These five words struck me and made me realize that I wasn't happy with where I was. I knew I needed to do something, but had no idea what. How? I had just quit my job. I needed to pay bills. Children are expensive! And when am I going to travel and experience different cultures, learn, and breathe in the beauty of places and people we met in different parts of the world again? It seemed like so long ago. My thoughts were cut off by Bob, yelling at me from my screen. "Most people coast along safely in life until they die!" Wow. That sentence slapped me in the face. I am turning 40 this year, and I had my answer. I want financial and time freedom. I want to help people around the world and do what I love. It resonates with me. I want to create my own identity, fulfill my dreams. The words "free" and "freedom" keep popping up in these lockdown times. It seems like the world is losing more and more freedom and I want to help people find it! I want to give so much love and provide so much help that I will feel out of breath. Bang!!! My world was turned inside out and upside down in that very moment. I thought of Winston Churchill, when he said, "If you find yourself in a hole, stop digging!" At that moment, I decided to hold on to the wheel very firmly and 'steer my ship' to my new destination.

See, I am still on an incredible journey and I feel I am finally moving toward my goal. I am growing every day and gaining awareness in all that I am doing. It is a phenomenal feeling. I see my destination/goal, but I do not know how I am going to get there. It is a challenging, fulfilling, and amazing state, as the more I understand the laws, the calmer the approach I take, and it all seems to happen the way it should. The important point is faith: you must have purpose and faith.

My teacher used to say, "The happiness is not in reaching the top; happiness is in the journey." It is all the obstacles we have to overcome while trying to succeed that makes us who we are. We become serene, wiser, stronger, more persistent and disciplined, and enjoy the truly magnificent life.

My Bible of the Masterminds is the reflection of my journey and my growth. It is the most important part of the staircase, raising my awareness, my consciousness. It is like climbing a rock. Faith and the vision of reaching the top are stronger than the fear of falling. By looking down and behind you, you see incredible beauty and feel a sense of achievement, and your confidence and terror barriers start disappearing. You feel the joy and bliss! "I am attracting more beautiful and helpful people and situations into my life and my mind is a center of divine operation and divine operation is always for expansion and fuller expression."

I must share a secret, as by doing so, I demonstrate the proof of manifestation of the best. I attracted Peggy McColl into my life. Peggy is a world-renowned wealth, business and manifestation expert as well as the New York Times best-selling author of many books. She is phenomenal, and she demands the best of herself and of everyone she does business with. She is a beautiful manifestation of her teaching. Her mindset is infectious and she has shown me how to apply her lessons. I am blessed and incredibly grateful for her. She helped me to 'give birth' to my first baby (this book), and without her, I feel I would be lost in the sea. She was sent to me with Trace as angels from heaven, spreading their wings and helping me to break my terror barrier. She gave me her complete author program as a gift because they believed in me! I willingly give, so I graciously received their amazing gift. I do not know how this happened, but everything happens for a reason. I believe, so I will succeed! I am deeply, profoundly grateful for everything coming to me in the process and appreciate all the abundance that is coming my way!

Alfred Adler once said, "I am grateful for the idea that has used me." My book is the idea that has used me. It is a combination of many powerful statements of masterminds, living or dead, and pictures from my life's adventures and blissful moments. Both are responsible for who I am today, a spirit made to perfection.

This book is my precious gift to you. May your awareness grow. Go and search for those whose powerful statements vibrate through your body. Listen to your intuition and inside voice, and follow it.

With love and deepest gratitude,

Vladimira Kuna

DAY 1

"A human being is a part of the whole
called by us universe, a part limited
in time and space.
He experiences himself, his thoughts
and feeling as something separated
from the rest, a kind of optical delusion
of his consciousness.
This delusion is a kind of prison for us,
restricting us to our personal desires
and to affection for a few persons
nearest to us.
Our task must be to free ourselves
from this prison by widening our circle
of compassion to embrace all living
creatures and the whole of nature
in its beauty."

~Albert Einstein

DAY 2

*"In times of change, learners inherit the earth,
while the learned find themselves beautifully equipped
to deal with a world that no longer exists."*

~ Eric Hoffer

"What you resist persists."

~Carl Jung

DAY 3

"You create your own universe as you go along."

~ Winston Churchill

*"Whether you think you can, or think you can't,
either way you are right."*

~ Henry Ford

DAY 4

"The starting point of all achievement is desire.
Keep this constantly in mind.
weak desire brings weak results,
just as a small fire makes a small
amount of heat."

~ Napoleon Hill

DAY 5

"The whole process of mental adjustment and atonement can be summed up in one word, Gratitude.
First, you believe that there is one Intelligent Substance, from which all things proceed;

Second, you believe that this Substance gives you everything you desire; and

Third, you relate yourself to it by a feeling of deep and Profound Gratitude."

~ Wallace D. Wattles

DAY 6

"Any idea, plan or purpose may be planted in the subconscious mind by repetition of thought empowered by faith and expectancy."

~ Bob Proctor

"Your brain operates in the present moment and if you tell it exciting and clear instructions—as if you're already there—the brain will have an ultimate sense of inevitability to provide you Everything you want."

~ Marisa Peer

DAY 7

"Decide what you want. Connect to yourself to feel what it is like to have it. Live like that, as if you already have it and you do not have to know how you are going to accomplish these things."

~ Bob Proctor

DAY 8

"There is enough for everyone.
If you believe it, if you can see it, if you can
act from it, it will show up for you.
That's the truth."

~ Michael Beckwith

DAY 9

"To believe in the things you can see and touch is no belief at all — but to believe in the unseen is a triumph and a blessing."

~ A. Lincoln

DAY 10

"Calmness of mind is one of the most beautiful jewels of wisdom. It is the result of long and patient effort in self-control. Its presence is an indication of ripened experience, and of a more than ordinary knowledge of the laws and operations of thought."

~ James Allen

"The cave you fear to enter holds the treasure you seek."

~ Joseph Campbell

DAY 11

"One half of knowing what you want is knowing what you must give up before you get it."

Sidney Howard

"I am so happy and grateful now that... every day, in every way, I feel fantastic!"

~ Bob Proctor

DAY 12

"Everything can be taken from a man
but one thing:
the last of the human freedoms –
to choose one's attitude
in any given set of circumstances,
to choose one's own way."

~ Viktor Frankl

DAY 13

*"And now here is my secret, a very simple secret:
It is only with the heart that one can see rightly;
what is essential is invisible to the eye."*

~ Antoine de Saint-Exupéry

DAY 14

"In absence of clearly defined goals, we become strangely loyal to performing daily trivia, until we ultimately become enslaved by it."

~ Robert Heinlein

"Destiny is no matter of chance. It is a matter of choice. It is not a thing to be waited for, it is a thing to be achieved."

~ William Jennings Bryan

"Integrity is the essence of everything successful."

~ R. Buckminster Fuller

"Be like a postage stamp. Stick to it until you get there."

~ Bob Proctor

DAY 15

"Riches do not respond to wishes. They respond to definite plans, backed by definite desires, through constant persistence."

~ Napoleon Hill

"The truth is you can do anything, but you've got to believe it. Without belief it is not going to happen."

~ Sandy Gallagher

DAY 16

"Vibrations never lie. A person could be saying one thing and yet, thinking another. Get to the point where you pay closer attention to the vibrations you are receiving rather than the words you are hearing. Intuition is one of the most valuable mental tools you possess.
Begin to consciously use it.
Your rewards will be worth the effort."

~ Bob Proctor

DAY 17

*"The intuitive mind is a sacred gift and the
rational mind is a faithful servant.
We have created a society that honors the servant
and has forgotten the gift."*

~Albert Einstein

DAY 18

"Faith is the bird that sings when the dawn is still dark."

~ Rabindranath Tagore

"All power is from within and therefore under our control."

~Robert Collier

DAY 19

"Dedicate your life to a cause that inspires you
and also greatly serves others.
Master plan your life. If you don't fill your day with high priorities,
it will automatically become filled with low priorities."

~John Frederick Demartini

DAY 20

*"I am so happy and grateful that
I am God's highest form of creation.*

*There never has been and there
never will be another person
created that will equal me!*

*I love my life. I am in control of my
life because I am in control of me.*

*I know that whatever happens
outside of me has no bearing
on who I am!"*

~Bob Proctor

DAY 21

*"There is one thing stronger than
all the armies of the world,
and that is an idea whose time has come."*

~ Victor Hugo

DAY 22

*"Many of life's failures are people
who did not realize how close they were
to success when they gave up."*

~ Thomas Edison

DAY 23

"When you appreciate what you have,
then you will receive more.
when you are in this moment feeling
gratitude for this moment, you actually up your
vibrational signal to attract more things
to be grateful for."

~ Joe Vitale

DAY 24

*"A man is what he thinks
about all day long."*

~ Ralph Waldo Emerson

*"People don't resist change; people
resist being changed!"*

~ Bob Proctor

DAY 25

"The fact is that
harnessing the power of your mind
can be more effective
than the drugs you have been
programmed to believe you need."

~ Bruce Lipton

DAY 26

"If you argue and rankle and contradict, you may achieve a victory sometimes; but it will be an empty victory because you will never get your opponent's good will."

~ Benjamin Franklin

"Our environment, the world in which we live and work, is a mirror of our attitudes and expectations. Your living is determined not so much by what life brings to you as by the attitude you bring to life; not so much by what happens to you as by the way your mind looks at what happens."

~ Bob Proctor

"The line between life or death is determined by what we are willing to do."

~ Bear Grylls

DAY 27

*"You are the master of your destiny. You can influence, direct
and control your own environment.
You can make your life
what you want it to be."*

~ Napoleon Hill

DAY 28

*"For a moment, acknowledge and honor
all that you are instead of all that you are not."*

~ Jim Kwik

*"The world doesn't pay you for what you know,
it pays you for what you do."*

~ Jack Canfield

DAY 29

"The universe will kick you out of your nest
so you can fly."

~ James Arthur Ray

DAY 30

"My current situation is not my final destination."

~ Lewis Howes

DAY 31

*"All human actions are motivated at their deepest level
by two emotions – fear or love.
In truth there are only two emotions
– only two words in the language of the soul…
Fear wraps our bodies in clothing, love allows us to stand naked.
Fear clings to and clutches all that we have,
love gives all that we have away.
Fear holds close, love holds dear.
Fear grasps, love lets go.
Fear rankles, love soothes.
Fear attacks, love amends."*

~ Neale Donald Walsch

DAY 32

*"Your mind responds to the pictures in
your head and the words you say to yourself."*

~ Marisa Peer

*"The universe will start to rearrange itself
to make it happen for you."*

~ Joe Vitale

DAY 33

*"Faith is an invisible and invincible magnet,
and attracts to itself whatever it fervently desires
and calmly and persistently expects."*

~ Ralph Waldo Trine

DAY 34

"See the things that you want as already yours. Know that they will come to you at need. Then let them come. Don't fret and worry about them. Don't think about your lack of them. Think of them as yours, as belonging to you, as already in your possession."

~ Robert Collier

DAY 35

*"There is a power which never fails to present
opportunity to the advancing man
who is moving in obedience to law.
God cannot help you if you act in a certain way;
He must do so in order to help himself."*

~ Wallace D. Wattles

DAY 36

*"The moment your belief matches with any state
you fuse with it,
and this union results in the activation
and projection of its plots, plans, conditions
and circumstances.
This new state of conscious awareness becomes
your home from which you view the world."*

~ Bob Proctor

DAY 37

"You get whatever you expect to get.
The only question is:
What do you want?"

~ Mark Victor Hansen

DAY 38

"Tempest-tossed souls, wherever you may be, under whatsoever conditions ye may live, know this — in the ocean of life the isles of Blessedness are smiling, and the sunny shore of your ideal awaits your coming.
Keep your hands firmly upon the helm of thought.
In the bark of your soul reclines the commanding Master;
He does but sleep; wake Him.
Self-control is strength;
Right Thought is mastery;
Calmness is power.
Say unto your heart,
'Peace be still!'"

~ James Allen

DAY 39

"You are the designer of your destiny.
You are the author.
You write the story.
The pen is in your hand, and the outcome
is whatever you choose."

~ Lisa Nichols

DAY 40

"I dream my painting, and then I paint my dream."

~ Vincent Van Gogh

"…It is your Father's pleasure to give you the kingdom,"

~ Jesus

DAY 41

"Whatsoever ye shall ask in prayer,
believing, ye shall receive."

~ Matthew 21:22

DAY 42

*"We have to do the best we can.
This is our sacred human responsibility."*

~ Albert Einstein

DAY 43

*"You have a fresh start any moment you choose,
for things we call 'failure' is not the falling down,
but the staying down."*

~ Mary Pickford

DAY 44

"...In order to love others,
first,
you need to love yourself."

~ Marisa Peer

DAY 45

*"Most folks are about as happy
as they make up their minds to be."*

~ Abraham Lincoln

"You cannot give what you have not got."

~ Horace

DAY 46

*"Whether the object of your faith is real or false, you will
get results. your subconscious mind responds to the thought
in your mind. look upon faith as a thought in your mind
and that will suffice.
Know that you can remake yourself by giving
a new blue print to your subconscious mind."*

~ Joseph Murphy

DAY 47

"The conscious use of this great power attracts to you greatly multiplied resources, intensifies your wisdom, and enables you to make use of advantages which you formerly failed to recognize.

In visualizing, or making a mental picture, you are not endeavoring to change the laws of nature."

~ Genevieve Behrend

"If passion drives you, let reason hold the reins."

~ Benjamin Franklin

DAY 48

"*A Paradigm is a mental program that has almost exclusive control over our habitual behavior and almost all of our behavior is habitual.*"

~ Bob Proctor

"*Success is the ability to go from one failure to another with no loss of enthusiasm.*"

~ Winston Churchill

"*I am so happy and grateful now that... I engage in exceptional thinking to achieve extraordinary results.*"

~ Bob Proctor

DAY 49

"The words you use will either minimize or maximize stress."

~ Marisa Peer

DAY 50

"If you don't take risks, you'll have a wasted soul."

~ Drew Barrymore

"Faith is the only known antidote to failure."

~ Napoleon Hill

DAY 51

"When you follow the dream in your heart,
you're energized, inspired, and motivated."

~ John Frederick Demartini

DAY 52

"When your idea is ready, no one's going to stop it from blooming."

~ Victor Hugo

*"Pay attention to how you feel.
That's what gratitude is all about."*

~ Sandy Gallagher

DAY 53

*"The secret of change
is to focus all of your energy,
not on fighting the old, but on building the new."*

~ Socrates

DAY 54

"I demand riches in definite terms;
I have a definite plan for acquiring riches;
I am engaged in carrying out my plan, and I am giving an equivalent,
in useful service, of the value of those riches I demand."

~ Andrew Carnegie

DAY 55

*"To look upon the appearance of poverty will produce
corresponding forms in your own mind.
Instead you must hold to the truth that there is no poverty.
There is only abundance."*

~ Wallace D. Wattles

DAY 56

"One of the most tragic things I know about human nature is that all of us tend to put off living. We are all dreaming of some magical rose garden over the horizon instead of enjoying the roses that are blooming outside our windows today."

~ Dale Carnegie

DAY 57

"Our greatest weakness lies in giving up. The most certain way to succeed is always to try just one more time."

~ Thomas Edison

"The only thing that can grow is the thing you give energy to."

~ Ralph Waldo Emerson

DAY 58

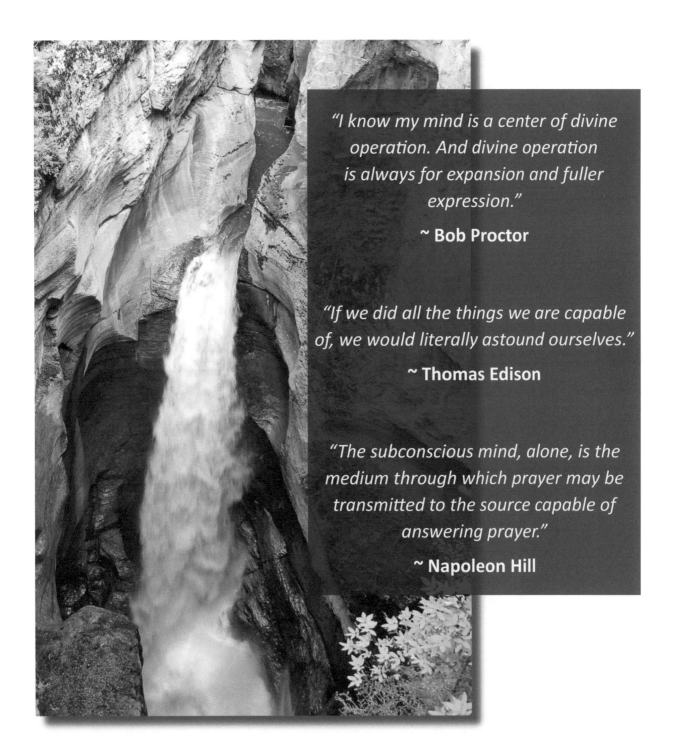

"I know my mind is a center of divine operation. And divine operation is always for expansion and fuller expression."

~ Bob Proctor

"If we did all the things we are capable of, we would literally astound ourselves."

~ Thomas Edison

"The subconscious mind, alone, is the medium through which prayer may be transmitted to the source capable of answering prayer."

~ Napoleon Hill

DAY 59

*"Strange and marvelous things will
happen with constant regularity as you alter
your life and begin in harmony with
the laws of the universe."*

~ Earl Nightingale

DAY 60

*"The greatest discovery of my generation
is that human beings can alter their lives
by altering their attitudes of mind."*

~ William James

DAY 61

"You don't have to slow down...calm down."

~ Bob Proctor

"The Divine operation is always for expansion and fuller expression."

~ Thomas Troward

DAY 62

"When I've gathered enough information to make a decision,
I don't take a vote, I make a decision."

~ Ronald Reagan

"People do not resist change, when it is their choice.
People resist being changed."

~ Michael Basch

DAY 63

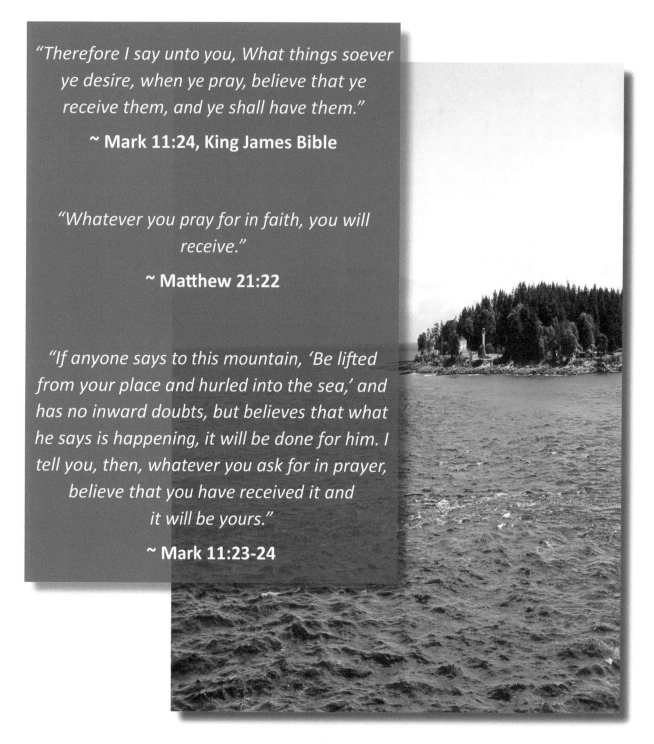

"Therefore I say unto you, What things soever ye desire, when ye pray, believe that ye receive them, and ye shall have them."

~ Mark 11:24, King James Bible

"Whatever you pray for in faith, you will receive."

~ Matthew 21:22

"If anyone says to this mountain, 'Be lifted from your place and hurled into the sea,' and has no inward doubts, but believes that what he says is happening, it will be done for him. I tell you, then, whatever you ask for in prayer, believe that you have received it and it will be yours."

~ Mark 11:23-24

DAY 64

"Observation is power;
judgment is weakness."

~ Leland Val Van De Wall

DAY 65

"Follow your passion,
And success will follow you."

~ Terri Guillemets

DAY 66

"Empty pockets never held anyone back.
Only empty heads and empty hearts can do that."

~ Norman Vincent Peale

"It is always too early to quit."

~ Norman Vincent Peale

DAY 67

"When one door closes another door opens; but we often look so long and so regretfully upon the closed door, that we do not see the ones which open for us."

~ Alexander Graham Bell

DAY 68

"When everything seems to be going against you, remember that the airplane takes off against the wind, not with it."

~ Henry Ford

DAY 69

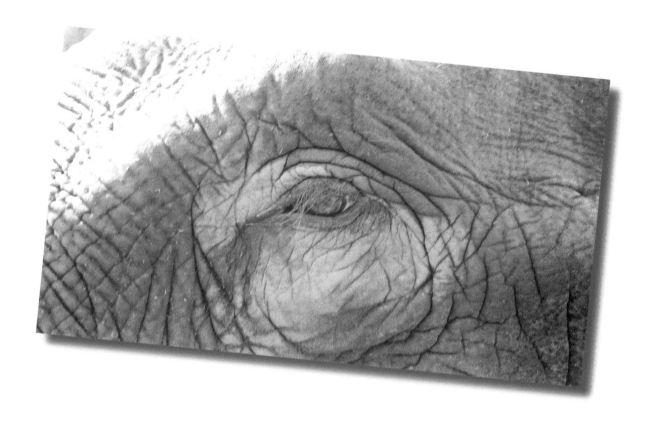

*"It's a human need to feel in control. But it's a complete fallacy.
There is no control. The only thing you can control is your thoughts.
Your thoughts control your feelings. Your feelings control your
actions. And your actions control your events. So if you
change your thinking, you change everything."*

~ Marisa Peer

DAY 70

"Nothing can stop the man with the right mental attitude from achieving his goal; nothing on earth can help the man with the wrong mental attitude."

~ Thomas Jefferson

DAY 71

"An educated person is a person who has so developed the faculties of their mind that they can acquire anything they want or its equivalent without violating the rights of others."

~ Socrates

DAY 72

"Sometimes, bad things that happen in our lives put us directly on a path to the most wonderful thing that will ever happen to us."

~ Nicole Reed

DAY 73

"The only thing you can attract to you are those things that are in harmonious vibration with you."

~ Bob Proctor

DAY 74

"Thought in the mind hath made us, what we are by thought was wrought and built.
If a man's mind hath evil thoughts, pain comes on him as comes the wheel the ox behind.
If one endure in purity of thought,
Joy follows him as his own shadow–sure."

~ James Allen

"Nothing is good or bad, except our thinking makes it so."

~ Ralph Waldo Trine

DAY 75

"No individual has sufficient experience,
Education, native ability, and knowledge
To ensure the accumulation of a great
Fortune without the cooperation
Of other people."

~ Napoleon Hill

DAY 76

"If you can find a path with no obstacles,
it probably doesn't lead anywhere."

~ Frank A. Clark

DAY 77

"You are your own highest authority. Do not place your source of authority outside of you.
Go within to see if the truth you've found is in harmony with the truth you find in your heart."

~ Neale Donald Walsch

DAY 78

"My Father is the ruler of all the world,
and is expressing His directing power through me."

~ Genevieve Behrend

DAY 79

"Everything is energy and that's all there is to it.
Match the frequency of the reality you want and
you cannot help but get that reality.
It can be no other way.
This is not philosophy.
This is physics."

~ Albert Einstein

DAY 80

*"That clear mental picture you must have continually
in mind, as the sailor has in mind the port toward
which he is sailing the ship;
you must keep your face toward it all the time.
You must no more lose sight of it than the steersman
loses sight of the compass."*

~ Wallace D. Wattles

DAY 81

*"To learn you need a certain degree
of confidence, not too much and not too little.
If you have too little confidence, you will think you can't learn.
If you have too much, you will think you don't have to learn."*

~ Eric Hoffer

DAY 82

"Books serve to show a man that those
original thoughts of his aren't
very new after all."

~ Abraham Lincoln

DAY 83

"I am so happy and grateful now that...
I am a 'fountain' to those
around me and myself
- a source of energy,
ideas, positivity and abundance."

~ Bob Proctor

DAY 84

"Obstacles are those frightful things you see when you take your eyes off your goal."

~ Henry Ford

"You always get what you consciously believe and expect."

~ Joe Vitale

DAY 85

"*Super successful people aren't the most gifted people in their fields.*

They just work, study and practice more than the competition."

~ Jack Canfield

DAY 86

"Hack your past with forgiveness.
Hack your present with mindfulness.
Hack your future with
I am enough."

~ Vishen Lakhiani

DAY 87

"I never mastered time management.
No one manages time; time cannot be managed.
I merely manage activities."

~ Earl Nightingale

DAY 88

"Imagination is more powerful
than knowledge.
Imagination is more powerful
than logic."

~ Marisa Peer

DAY 89

"I love life because what more is there?"

~ Anthony Hopkins

"Act as if it were impossible to fail."

~ Dorothea Brande

DAY 90

"It is in your moments of decision that your destiny is shaped."

~ Anthony Robbins

DAY 91

"Quality is not an act, it is a habit."

~ Aristotle

"If you set your goals ridiculously high and it's a failure, you will fail above everyone else's success."

~ James Cameron

"What you want, wants you, and what you are moving towards is moving towards you."

~ Marisa Peer

DAY 92

*"Do you live in a minefield
or a garden?
When we live in a minefield
mentality,
We explode with the weeds of
worry, doubt, fear, lack, and
limitation.
Choose to cultivate your inner
garden!"*

~ Michael Beckwith

*"I am so happy and grateful
now that...
I continuously stretch myself
To create a life that is free
from regret."*

~ Bob Proctor

DAY 93

"I am a creative genius!
I am worthy of everything I desire!
I am in love with my life!"

~ Dr. Joe Dispenza

DAY 94

"There is one quality which one must possess to win,
and that is definiteness of purpose,
the knowledge of what one wants,
and a burning desire to possess it."

~ Napoleon Hill

DAY 95

"The strong, calm man is always loved and revered. He is like a shade-giving tree in a thirsty land, or a sheltering rock in a storm. Who does not love a tranquil heart, a sweet-tempered, balanced life?"

~ James Allen

DAY 96

"*If you train yourself in the practice of deliberately picturing your desire and carefully examining your picture you will soon find that your thoughts and desires proceed in a more orderly procession than ever before.*"

~ Genevieve Behrend

DAY 97

"The way you start anything will determine how you finish. Start your week with purpose."

~ Gena West

DAY 98

"I am so happy and grateful now that
I walk to and through my fears
so i can achieve my goals and
live my dreams.
Bob Proctor

DAY 99

"An unexamined life is not worth living."

~ Socrates

DAY 100

"The grateful mind is constantly fixed upon the best;
therefore it tends to become the best;
it takes the form or character of the best,
and will receive the best."

~ Wallace D. Wattles

DAY 101

"Man is the individualized expression or reflection of God imaged forth and made manifest in bodily form.

How is it, then, I hear it asked, that man has the limitations that he has, that he is subject to fears and forebodings, that he is subject to fears and forebodings, that he is liable to sin and error, that he is the victim of disease and suffering? There is but one reason. He is not living, expect in rare cases here and there, in the conscious realization of his own true Being, and hence of his own true Self."

~ Ralph Waldo Trine

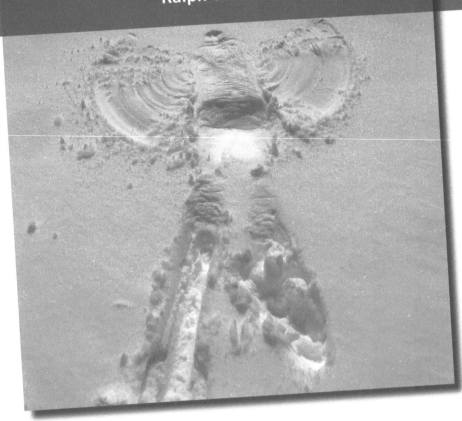

DAY 102

*"Surround yourself with only people
who are going to lift you higher."*

~ Oprah Winfrey

DAY 103

"Life beats down and crushes the soul and art reminds you that you have one."

~ **Stella Adler**

DAY 104

"FOCUS is not something you have,
it is something you do."

~ Jim Kwik

"Change is difficult but often
essential to survival."

~ Les Brown

DAY 105

"The man who acquires the ability to take full possession of his own mind may take possession of anything else to which he is justly entitled."

~ Andrew Carnegie

DAY 106

"Time is really the only capital that any human being has, and the only thing he can't afford to lose."

~ Thomas Edison

DAY 107

"Concentrate all your thoughts upon the work at hand. the sun's rays do not burn until brought to a focus."

~ Alexander Graham Bell

DAY 108

"Time is a companion who goes with us on a journey and reminds us to cherish every moment, because it will never come again. What we leave behind is not as important as how we have lived."

~ Jean-Luc Picard

DAY 109

"When we are grateful,
Fear disappears and abundance appears."

~ Tony Robbins

DAY 110

"The major reason for setting a goal is for what it makes of you to accomplish it. What it makes of you will always be the far greater value than what you get."

~ Jim Rohn

DAY 111

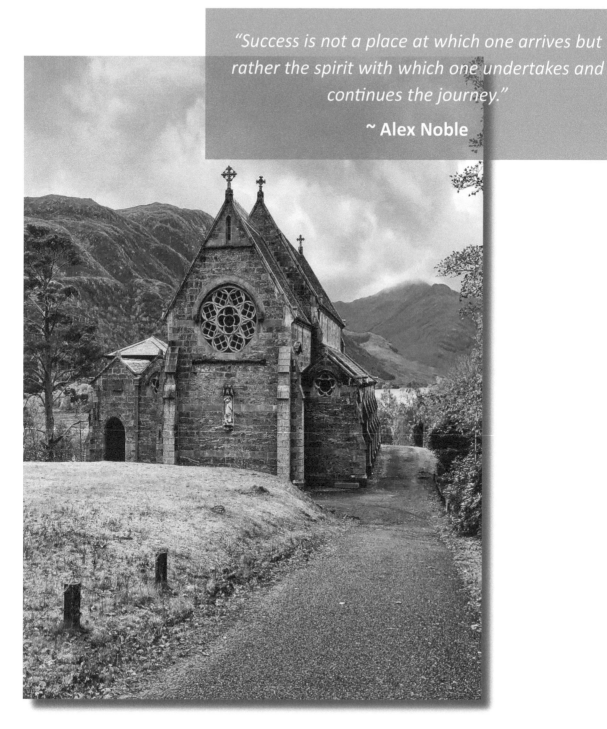

"*Success is not a place at which one arrives but rather the spirit with which one undertakes and continues the journey.*"

~ Alex Noble

DAY 112

*"I am so happy and grateful now that...
I continuously stretch myself to create a life that is above and beyond anything I have experienced in the past."*

~ Bob Proctor

*"When defeat comes, accept it as a signal
that your plans are not sound, rebuild those plans, and set sail once more towards your coveted goal."*

~ Napoleon Hill

DAY 113

"To be able to shape your future,
you have to be willing and able to change
your paradigm."

~ Joel Barker

DAY 114

*"Shoot for the moon. Even if you miss,
you will land among the stars."*

~ Les Brown

DAY 115

*"You never change things by fighting
the existing reality.
To change something, build a new model that makes
the existing model obsolete."*

~ R. Buckminster Fuller

DAY 116

"If you don't have some self-doubts and fears when you pursue a dream, then you haven't dreamed big enough."

~ Joe Vitale

DAY 117

*"Every thought you think and every word you say
forms a blueprint and your mind
must work to make that blueprint real."*

~ Marisa Peer

DAY 118

"Condemnation without investigation is the highest form of ignorance."

~ Albert Einstein

DAY 119

"Coming together is a beginning, staying together is progress, and working together is success."

~ Henry Ford

"By giving people the power to share, we're making the world more transparent."

~ Mark Zuckerberg

DAY 120

"Gratitude is the single most important ingredient
to living a successful and fulfilled life."

~ Jack Canfield

DAY 121

*"Success is the
Progressive realization
Of a worthy ideal."*

~ Earl Nightingale

DAY 122

"Stand up to your obstacles and do something about them.
You will find that they haven't half the strength
you think they have."

~ Norman Vincent Peale

DAY 123

"There are no accidents in my philosophy.
Every effect must have its cause.
The past is the cause of the present,
and the present will be the cause of the future.
All these are links in the endless chain
stretching from the finite to the infinite."

~ Abraham Lincoln

DAY 124

*"I alone cannot change the world,
but I can cast a stone across the water
to create many ripples."*

~ Mother Teresa

DAY 125

*"Nothing is impossible, the word itself says,
'I'm possible!'"*

~ Audrey Hepburn

"If it ain't fun, don't do it!"

~ Jack Canfield

DAY 126

*"We are only limited by weakness of attention
and poverty of imagination!"*

~ Bob Proctor

DAY 127

*"My life is a glorious celebration
of the Living Christ!*

*Today I am reborn in the
awareness of my great
and mighty destiny!*

*Miracles occur in the field of my
beholding consciousness!*

*I am an agent for spiritual
advancement on this planet!*

*My acts of generosity quicken
the flow of abundance
in my life!*

*In the spirit of gratitude, I live
these words of truth!*

And so it is! Amen!"

~Michael Beckwith

DAY 128

*"The greater energy you can create through
the elevated emotions of the heart, the more
you are going to connect with the unified field, which means you are going to
experience more wholeness, connection, and oneness."*

~ Dr. Joe Dispenza

DAY 129

*"A person's right to life means his right to have
the free and unrestricted use of all the things
spiritual and physical unfolding –
in other words, his right to be rich."*

~ Wallace D. Wattles

DAY 130

"Before anything else, preparation is the key to success."

~ Alexander Graham Bell

DAY 131

"No matter how many mistakes you make or how slow you progress, you are still way ahead of everyone who isn't trying."

~ Tony Robbins

DAY 132

*"Learn to motivate
others by example."*

~ Napoleon Hill

DAY 133

"There may be no heroic connotation to the word 'persistence,' but the quality is to character what carbon is to steel."

~ Napoleon Hill

DAY 134

"Every act you have ever performed since the day you were born was performed because you wanted something."

~ Andrew Carnegie

DAY 135

"Use your headphones to reprogram your mind!"

~ Bruce Lipton

"Live your life and forget about your age."

~ Norman Vincent Peale

DAY 136

*"It is only when we get kicked down that we see
what we are made of. it's easy to be positive when everything
is going well, but the heart
of all great endeavors is the ability to stagger back to our
feet and keep moving forward,
however grim it gets."*

~ Bear Grylls

DAY 137

"*When you have exhausted all possibilities, remember this: you haven't.*"

~ Thomas Edison

DAY 138

"Inspiration gives you desire. Decision makes it an intention. Action makes it real."

~ Joe Vitale

"We are what we repeatedly do. Excellence, then, is not an act, but a habit."

~ Aristotle

DAY 139

*"Anyone who stops learning is old, whether at twenty or eighty.
Anyone who keeps learning stays young.
The greatest thing in life is to keep your mind young."*

~ Henry Ford

DAY 140

"I know not how to aid you, save in the assurance of one of mature age, and much severe experience, that you can not fail, if you resolutely determine, that you will not."

~ **Abraham Lincoln**

DAY 141

"Education is the kindling of a flame, not the filling of a vessel."

~ Socrates

DAY 142

*"Gratitude is a powerful process for shifting your energy
and bringing more of what you want into your life.
Be grateful for what you already have
and you will attract more good things."*

~ Bob Proctor

DAY 143

"As you're visualizing, you will know you have reached a 'Perfect Match Position' when you really feel connected to your demand and you know for certain it is anchoring in, not as a possibility, but as a fact.
It is already done."

~ Peggy McColl

DAY 144

"Learn to make every turn on the road.
Just because the road bends, does not mean it ends.
It is when you fail to make the turn, you reached the end."

~ Vladimira Kuna

DAY 145

*"I am grateful for
the idea that has used me."*

~ Alfred Adler

DAY 146

"Nothing in this world is worth having or worth doing
unless it means effort, pain, difficulty...
I have never in my life envied a human being who led an easy life;
I have envied a great many people who led difficult lives
and led them well."

~ Theodore Roosevelt

DAY 147

"Be faithful in small things because
It is in them that your strength lies."

~ Mother Teresa

DAY 148

"You don't learn to walk by following rules.
You learn by doing, and by falling over."

~ Richard Branson

DAY 149

"Twenty years from now you will be more disappointed by the things that you didn't do than by the ones you did do.
So, throw off the bowlines. Sail away from the safe harbor.
Catch the trade winds in your sails.
Explore. Dream. Discover."

~ Mark Twain

DAY 150

*"There are no limitations to the mind
except those that we acknowledge."*

~ Napoleon Hill

DAY 151

"People who are unable to motivate themselves must be content with mediocrity, no matter how impressive their other talents."

~ Andrew Carnegie

DAY 152

"You miss 100% of the shots you don't take."

~ Wayne Gretzky

DAY 153

"First, have a definite, clear practical ideal; a goal, an objective.
Second, have the necessary means to achieve your ends;
wisdom, money, materials, and methods.
Third, adjust all your means to that end."

~ Aristotle

DAY 154

"If you look at what you have in life, you'll always have more.
If you look at what you don't have in life, you'll never have enough."

~ Oprah Winfrey

DAY 155

*"I am so happy and grateful that
everything in my life is moving forward
in harmony with God's laws."*

~ Bob Proctor

DAY 156

"I would rather die of passion than of boredom."

~ Vincent van Gogh

*"If you're offered a seat on a rocket ship,
don't ask what seat! Just get on."*

~ Sheryl Sandberg

DAY 157

*"I didn't fail the test, I just found 100 ways
to do it wrong."*

~ Benjamin Franklin

DAY 158

"I have learned over the years that when one's mind is made up, this diminishes fear."

~ Rosa Parks

"It does not matter how slowly you go as long as you do not stop."

~ Confucius

DAY 159

"Too many of us are not living our dreams because we are living our fears."

~ Les Brown

DAY 160

"The spirit which sleeps in the mineral, breathes in the vegetable, moves in the animal and reaches its highest development in man is the Universal Mind, and it behooves us to span the gulf between being and doing, theory and practice, by demonstrating our understanding of the dominion which we have been given."

~ Charles F. Haanel

DAY 161

"Belief without talent can take you further than talent without belief. But when you have both, you're unstoppable."

~ Marisa Peer

DAY 162

*"Stop focusing on how stressed you are
and remember how blessed you are."*

~ Debbie Siebers

DAY 163

*"We are bound and connected by an invisible field of energy,
and this energy field can affect everyone's behaviors, emotional states,
and conscious and unconscious thoughts."*

~ Dr. Joe Dispenza

DAY 164

"I am telling you that your perception of ultimate reality is
more limited than you thought, and that
truth is more unlimited than you can imagine."

~ Neale Donald Walsch

DAY 165

*"While trying to find a solution,
sometimes problems solve themselves..."*

~ Mirela Sula

DAY 166

"When you give yourself permission to follow your curiosity, new ideas will come to you and doorways of opportunity will open for you."

~ Mary Morrissey

DAY 167

"I don't think of all the misery, but of the beauty that still remains."

~ Anne Frank

"Believe you can and you're halfway there."

~ Theodore Roosevelt

DAY 168

"Knowledge is only potential power.
It becomes power only when, and if, it is organized into
definite plans of action,
and directed to a definite end."

~ Napoleon Hill

DAY 169

"Opportunity is missed by most people because it is dressed in overalls and looks like work."

~ **Thomas Edison**

DAY 170

"To find yourself, think for yourself."

~ Socrates

"The path to success is to take massive, determined action."

~ Tony Robbins

DAY 171

*"Set a goal to achieve something that is so big,
so exhilarating that it excites you and scares
you at the same time."*

~ Bob Proctor

*"Visioneering is where you truly begin to create your world,
and you do it through the effective use of your higher faculties."*

~ Sandy Gallagher

DAY 172

*"Everybody is a genius. But if you judge a fish
by its ability to climb a tree, it will live its whole life
believing that it is stupid."*

~ Albert Einstein

DAY 173

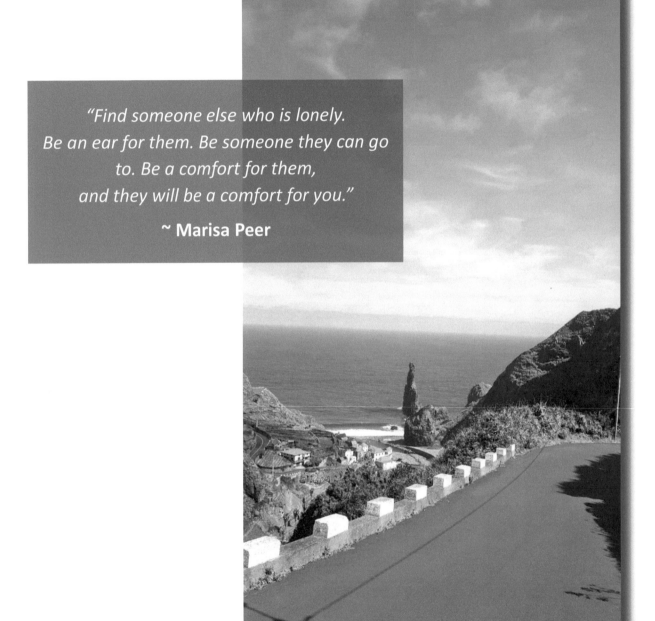

*"Find someone else who is lonely.
Be an ear for them. Be someone they can go
to. Be a comfort for them,
and they will be a comfort for you."*

~ Marisa Peer

DAY 174

"You must lay aside your greed; have no unworthy motive
in your desire to become rich and powerful.
It is legitimate and right to desire riches, if you
want them for the sake of your soul, but not if you desire
them for the lists of the flesh."

~ Wallace D. Wattles

DAY 175

"Nothing can prevent your picture
from coming into concrete form except
the same power which gave it birth – yourself."

~ Genevieve Behrend

DAY 176

"If you want to be happy,
set a goal that commands your thoughts,
liberates your energy,
and inspires your hopes."

~ Andrew Carnegie

DAY 177

"The most successful men in the end are those whose success is the result of steady accretion."

~ Alexander Graham Bell

"Happiness is when what you think, what you say, and what you do are in harmony."

~ Mahatma Gandhi

DAY 178

"Thinking is the hardest work there is, which is probably the reason why so few engage in it."

~ Henry Ford

DAY 179

"Do not be embarrassed by your failures, learn from them and start again."

~ Richard Branson

DAY 180

"You will be what you will to be;
Let failure find its false content
In that poor word, 'environment,'
But spirit scorns it, and is free.

It masters time, it conquers space;
It cows that boastful trickster, Chance,
And bids the tyrant Circumstance
Uncrown, and fill a servant's place.

The human Will, that force unseen,
The offspring of deathless Soul,
Can hew a way to any goal,
Though walls of granite intervene.

Be not impatient in delay,
But wait as one who understands;
When spirit rises and commands,
The gods are ready to obey."

~ James Allen

DAY 181

"I believe that you can always reach your goal when you see it with your vision, feel it with your heart filled with love and gratitude.
Trust your intuition and have faith to take action.
'How', will happen itself."

~ Vladimira Kuna

DAY 182

*"You don't decide what your purpose is in life, you discover it.
Your purpose is your reason for living."*

~ Bob Proctor

DAY 183

*"The greatest wealth
is to live content with little."*

~ **Plato**

*"Storms draw something out of us
what calm seas don't."*

~ **Peggy McColl**

DAY 184

"Wisely, and slow.
They stumble
that run fast."

~ William Shakespeare

DAY 185

*"The greatest glory in living lies not in never falling,
but in rising every time we fall."*

~ Nelson Mandela

"The way to get started is to quit talking and begin doing."

~ Walt Disney

DAY 186

"Understand that the creative process is always flowing to and through you. it is your thoughts that are shaping that energy. Always have the picture of what you want in your mind."

~ Sandy Gallagher

DAY 187

"The purpose of our lives is to be happy."

~ Dalai Lama

*"Life is what happens when you're busy
Making other plans."*

~ John Lennon

DAY 188

*"Live in the sunshine, swim the sea,
drink the wild air."*

~ Ralph Waldo Emerson

DAY 189

"Human nature will not change. In any future great national trial, compared with the men of this, we shall have as weak and as strong, as silly and as wise, as bad and as good."

~ Abraham Lincoln

DAY 190

*"A hero is anyone who devotes their life to
contribution, anyone who is inspired to
set an example, anyone who feels guided to serve something
greater than themselves."*

~ Tony Robbins

DAY 191

"Nothing in life is to be feared,
it is only to be understood.
Now is the time to understand more,
so that we may fear less."

~ Marie Curie

DAY 192

*"I am constantly thinking,
talking and writing
about the reality
I want to create."*

~ Jack Canfield

DAY 193

"Don't let your circumstances hold you back
from your dreams.
you have the power to overcome
anything and become
who you envision yourself being!"

~ Lewis Howes

DAY 194

*"It's not enough to change your state of being only when you mediate.
It's not sufficient to just think and feel peace with your eyes closed,
and then open them and carry on throughout the day in limited,
unconscious states of mind and body."*

~ Dr. Joe Dispenza

DAY 195

"The way you feel about anything comes down to two things: the pictures you make in your head and the words you say to yourself."

~ Marisa Peer

DAY 196

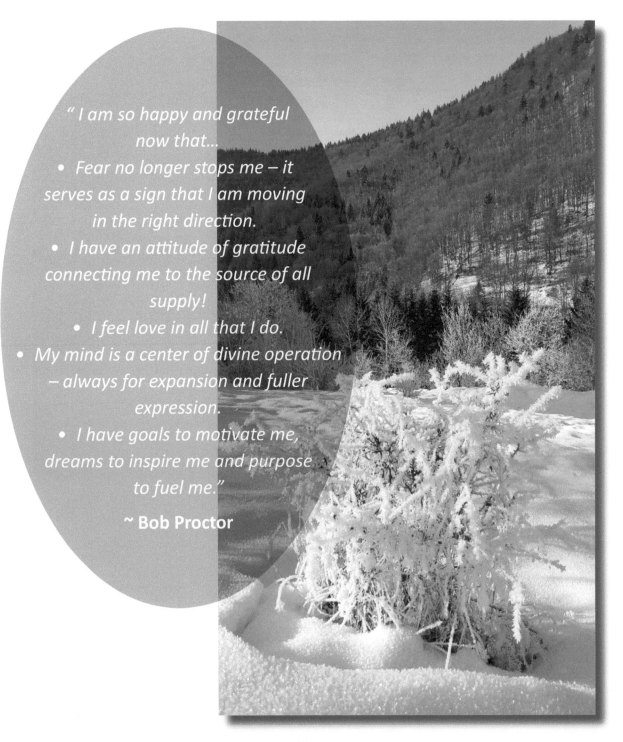

" I am so happy and grateful
now that...
• Fear no longer stops me – it
serves as a sign that I am moving
in the right direction.
• I have an attitude of gratitude
connecting me to the source of all
supply!
• I feel love in all that I do.
• My mind is a center of divine operation
– always for expansion and fuller
expression.
• I have goals to motivate me,
dreams to inspire me and purpose
to fuel me."

~ Bob Proctor

DAY 197

"The secret of success is to do the common thing uncommonly well."

~ John D. Rockefeller Jr.

*"There is no other road to genius
Than through voluntary self-effort."*

~ Napoleon Hill

DAY 198

*"The secret of success lies not in doing your own work
but in recognizing the best person to do it."*

~ Andrew Carnegie

DAY 199

"What do you focus on most of the time?
What do you think about most of the time?
Are you focusing on rich thoughts or poverty thoughts?"

~ Peggy McColl

"Failure is
simply the opportunity to begin again,
This time more intelligently."

~ Henry Ford

DAY 200

"I can see clearly now the rain is gone.
I can see all obstacles in my way.
Gone are the dark clouds that had me blind.
It's gonna be a bright sunshiny day."

~ Johnny Nash

DAY 201

*"The trouble with most of us is that we would rather
be ruined by praise than saved by criticism."*

~ Norman Vincent Peale

DAY 202

"If you focus upon whatever you want,
you will attract whatever you want.
If you focus upon the lack of whatever you want,
you will attract more of the lack."

~ Esther Hicks

DAY 203

"Once you begin to look at what you really love to do with your time and your talent, ideas will start to come to you."

~ Mary Morrissey

DAY 204

"You are what you think about,
so be very careful to keep your thoughts positive
and on your goal."

~ Napoleon Hill

DAY 205

"The future depends on what we do in the present."
~ Mahatma Gandhi

"One thing I only know, and that is
that I know nothing."

~ **Socrates**

DAY 206

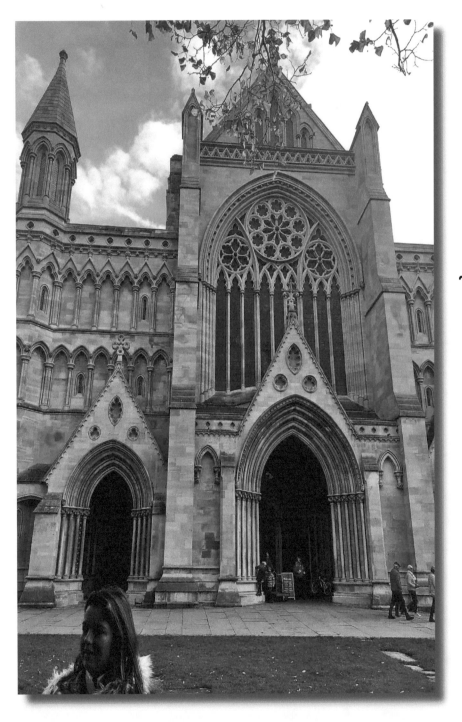

"The very best thing you can do for the whole world is to make the most of yourself."

~ Wallace D. Wattles

DAY 207

"The struggle ends when the gratitude begins.
The search is over when the finding starts.
And the finding is not a finding at all, but a creating.
You cannot find what you have been struggling for,
But you can create it.
And the jump-start of creation is gratitude."

~ Neale Donald Walsch

DAY 208

*"It is not what you want that you
attract, you attract what you believe to be true."*

~ Neville Goddard

DAY 209

"That some achieve great success,
Is proof to all that others can achieve it as well."

~ Abraham Lincoln

DAY 210

"Secrets to success lie not only in what people do, but also in what makes them do it."

~ Bob Proctor

DAY 211

*"You need to put your effort into falling in love with you
and then the world will change so dramatically."*

~ Marisa Peer

DAY 212

"The optimist is right.
The pessimist is right.
Point of view is the determining factor
In the life of each."

~ Ralph Waldo Trine

DAY 213

"Energy flows where attention goes."

~ Michael Beckwith

"If the glass is greener somewhere else...
Start watering your own lawn!"

~ Michael Beckwith

DAY 214

"When you get into a right place,
and everything goes against you
till it seems as if you couldn't hold on a minute longer,
never give up then,
for that's just the place and time that
the tide will turn."

~ Harriet Beecher Stowe

DAY 215

"Setting goals is the first step in turning the invisible into the visible."

~ Tony Robbins

DAY 216

"The greatest achievement was at first and for a time a dream. The oak sleeps in the acorn; the bird waits in the egg; and in the highest vision of a soul a waking angel stirs. Dreams are the seedlings of realities."

~ James Allen

DAY 217

"Abundance to me means being able to check off all those dreams that you had in life as a little kid."

~ Vishen Lakhiani

DAY 218

"No man will make a great leader who wants to do it all himself, or to get all the credit for doing it."

~ Andrew Carnegie

DAY 219

"The most costly words in the English language are 'I don't have time.'
You can budget your time correctly to have time for all your needs."

~ Napoleon Hill

DAY 220

*"Strong reasons make
Strong actions."*

~ William Shakespeare

DAY 221

"I haven't failed. I've just found 10,000 ways that won't work."

~ Thomas Edison

"Change the changeable, accept the unchangeable, and remove yourself from the unacceptable."

~ Denis Waitley

DAY 222

"How wonderful it is that nobody need wait a single moment before starting to improve the world."

~ Anne Frank

DAY 223

"Thoughts become things. If you see it in your mind,
you will hold it in your hand."

~ Bob Proctor

DAY 224

"Connect with your soul and ask to be guided."

~ Marie Diamond

DAY 225

*"The first rule of your mind is, what you expect you realize,
so expect amazing things."*

~ Marisa Peer

DAY 226

"The only man who never makes mistakes
is the man who never does anything."

~ Theodore Roosevelt

DAY 227

"A thought is a substance, producing the thing that is imagined by the thought."

~ Wallace D. Wattles

DAY 228

"Throw your heart over the fence and the rest will follow."

~ Norman Vincent Peale

"Either you run the day,
Or the day runs you."

~ Peggy McColl

DAY 229

"Educating the mind without educating the heart is no education at all."

~ Aristotle

DAY 230

*"And in the end it is not the years in your life that count,
it's the life in your years."*

~ Abraham Lincoln

DAY 231

*"I am not what **happened** to me,*
*I am what I **choose** to become."*

~ Carl Jung

DAY 232

"The only person with whom you have to compare yourself is you in the past."

~ Sigmund Freud

DAY 233

"You cannot teach a man anything.
You can only help him discover it within himself."

~ Galileo Galilei

DAY 234

"The greatest good you can do for another
Is not just to share your riches
But to reveal to him his own."

~ Benjamin Disraeli

DAY 235

"You cannot transit wisdom and insight to another person. The seed is already there. A good teacher touches the seed, allowing it to wake up, to sprout, and to grow."

~ Thich Nhat Hanh

DAY 236

"If you want to be happy, praise yourself a lot."

~ Marisa Peer

"If I have seen further it is by standing on the shoulders of giants."

~ Isaac Newton

DAY 237

"Courage is what it takes to stand up and speak. Courage is also what it takes to sit down and listen."

~ Winston Churchill

DAY 238

*"I am so happy and grateful now that...
I know my mind is a center of divine
operation and divine operation is
always for expansion and fuller
expression."*

~ Bob Proctor

DAY 239

"You are the first example of how people treat you."

~ Lisa Nichols

DAY 240

"Fear is NOT real – it is simply your 'old self' crying out in attempt to trick you back into your old ways of doing things."

~ Peggy McColl

"All impulses of thought have a tendency to clothe themselves in their physical equivalent."

~ Napoleon Hill

DAY 241

"An eye for an eye only ends up making the whole world blind."

~ Mahatma Gandhi

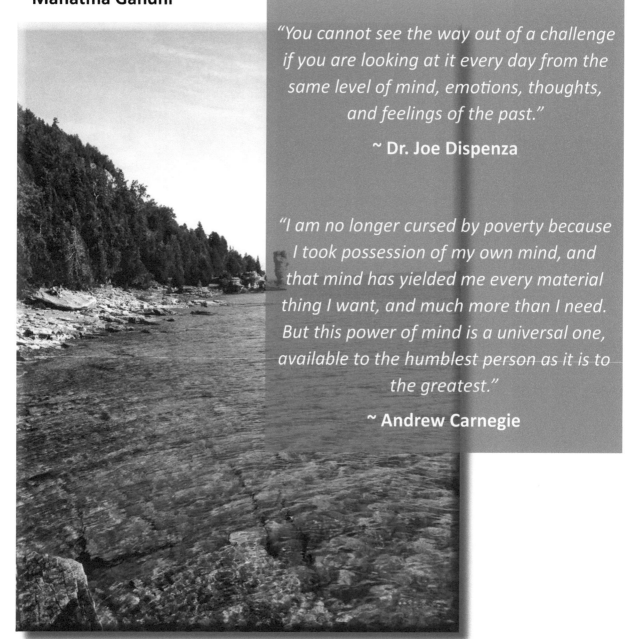

"You cannot see the way out of a challenge if you are looking at it every day from the same level of mind, emotions, thoughts, and feelings of the past."

~ Dr. Joe Dispenza

"I am no longer cursed by poverty because I took possession of my own mind, and that mind has yielded me every material thing I want, and much more than I need. But this power of mind is a universal one, available to the humblest person as it is to the greatest."

~ Andrew Carnegie

DAY 242

"Show me a successful individual and I'll show you someone who had real positive influences in his or her life. I don't care what you do for a living – if you do it well I'm sure there was someone cheering you on or showing the way. A mentor."

~ Denzel Washington

DAY 243

"Happiness may come from gaining things.
But true fulfilment comes from giving things.
Give, contribute, share – you become happy
when you make others happy."

~ Vishen Lakhiani

DAY 244

*"You cannot hope to build a better world without improving the individuals.
To that end, each of us must work
For our own improvement."*

~ Marie Curie

DAY 245

"The outer conditions of a person's life will always be found to be harmoniously related to his inner state...
Men do not attract that which they want, but that which they are."

~ James Allen

DAY 246

*"The world doesn't belong to leaders.
The world belongs to all humanity."*

~ Dalai Lama

*"Our chief want in life is somebody who
will make us do what we can."*

~ Ralph Waldo Emerson

DAY 247

"Decide what it is you want, write it down, review it constantly, and each day do something that moves you toward those goals."

~ Jack Canfield

"Be around people who can keep your energy and inspiration high. While you can make progress alone, it's so much easier when you have support."

~ Joe Vitale

DAY 248

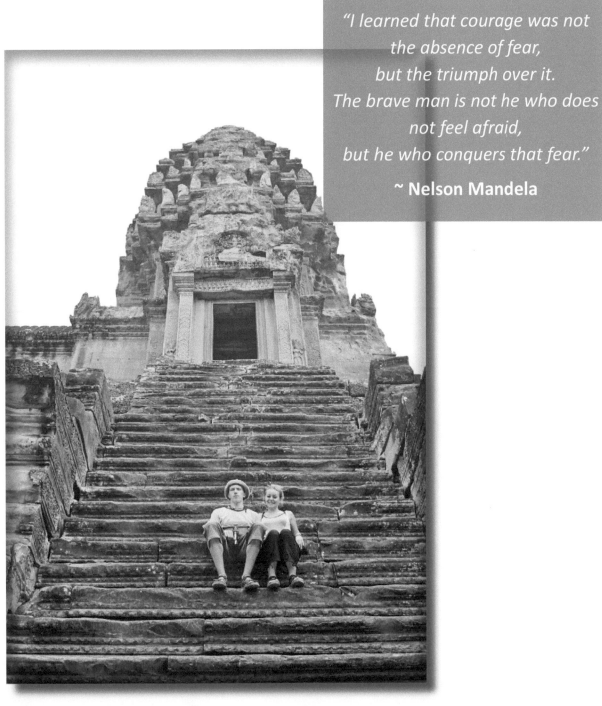

"*I learned that courage was not the absence of fear, but the triumph over it. The brave man is not he who does not feel afraid, but he who conquers that fear.*"

~ Nelson Mandela

DAY 249

"Great discoveries and improvements invariably involve the cooperation of many minds."

~ Alexander Graham Bell

DAY 250

"The deepest secret is that life is not a process of discovery, but a process of creation. You are not discovering yourself, but creating yourself anew. Seek therefore, not to find out Who You Are, but seek to determine Who You Want to Be."

~ Neale Donald Walsch

DAY 251

"An unresolved past never really goes away until you find the courage to revisit all the pain and accept that there's nothing you can do to change the past. What's happened has happened, and what's done is done."

~ Wallace D. Wattles

DAY 252

*"The only competition you will ever face
is with your own ignorance."*

~ Bob Proctor

"The only limits in our life are those we impose on ourselves."

~ Bob Proctor

DAY 253

"We can change our lives.
We can do, have, and be exactly what we wish."

~ Tony Robbins

"I challenge you to make your life a masterpiece.
I challenge you to join the ranks of those people
Who live what they teach, who walk their talk."

~ Tony Robbins

DAY 254

"Form a partnership with your brain, communicate with it better."

~ Marisa Peer

DAY 255

"If everyone is moving forward together, then success takes care of itself."

~ Henry Ford

DAY 256

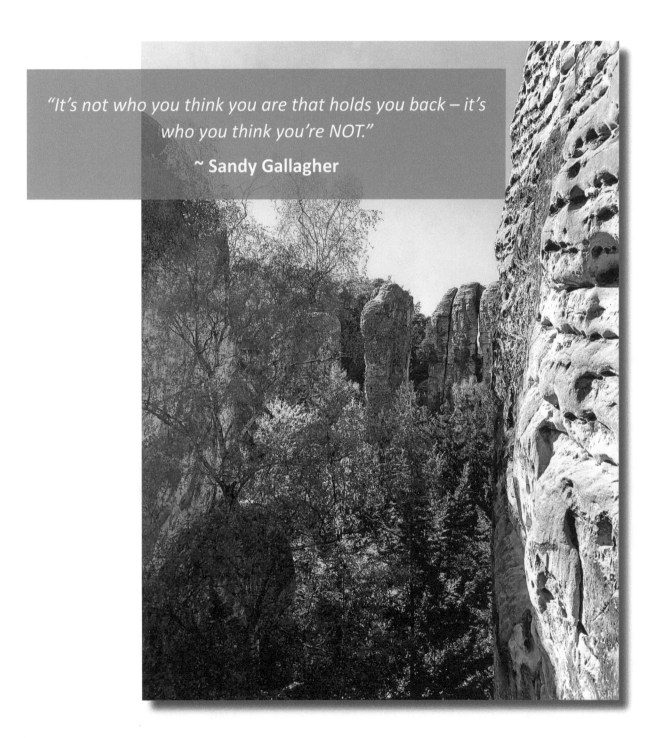

"It's not who you think you are that holds you back – it's who you think you're NOT."

~ Sandy Gallagher

DAY 257

*"You have to do your own growing
no matter how tall your grandfather was."*

~ Abraham Lincoln

DAY 258

*"Everything must have its beginning in mind.
The idea must contain within itself the only one
and primary substance there is,
and this means money as well as everything else."*

~ Genevieve Behrend

DAY 259

"You can break yourself free from your hereditary patterns, cultural codes, social beliefs; and prove once and for all that the power within you is greater than the power that's in the world."

~ Michael Beckwith

DAY 260

"People are not paid for what they know.
They are paid for what they do with what they know."

~ Napoleon Hill

DAY 261

"Accountability is the glue that ties commitment to the result."

~ Bob Proctor

DAY 262

"I never did anything by accident,
nor did any of my inventions come
by accident; they came by work."

~ Thomas Edison

DAY 263

"Spread love everywhere you go.
Let no one ever come to you without leaving happier."

~ Mother Teresa

"Survival can be summed up in three words
NEVER GIVE UP.
That's the heart of it really. Just keep trying."

~ Bear Grylls

DAY 264

*"Only a life lived for others is
a life worthwhile."*

~ Albert Einstein

DAY 265

"Courage is resistance to fear,
mastery of fear,
not absence of fear."
~ Mark Twain

DAY 266

"Between stimulus and response there is a space.
In that space is the power to choose our response.
In our response lies our growth and our freedom."

~ Peggy McColl

DAY 267

"Think like a queen.
A queen is not afraid to fail.
Failure is another steppingstone to greatness."

~ Oprah Winfrey

DAY 268

*"Love many things, for therein lies true strength,
and whosoever loves much performs much, and can accomplish much, and
what is done in love is done well."*

~ Vincent van Gogh

DAY 269

"The degree to which a person can grow is directly proportional to the amount of truth he can accept about himself without running away."

~ Leland Val Van De Wall

DAY 270

"People inspire you, or they drain you.
Pick them wisely."

~ Les Brown

"People are more comfortable with a familiar discomfort
than they are with an unfamiliar new possibility."

~ Lisa Nichols

DAY 271

"Tell me and I forget.
Teach me and I may
remember.
Involve me and I learn."

~ Benjamin Franklin

DAY 272

*"When I am working on a problem, I never think about beauty
but when I have finished, if the solution is not beautiful,
I know it is wrong."*

~ R. Buckminster Fuller

DAY 273

"When the voice and the vision on the inside is more
profound, and more clear and loud than all opinions on
the outside, you've begun to master your life."

~ John Frederick Demartini

DAY 274

*"Changing our perception
allows us to increase
our abundance set point."*

~ Mary Morrissey

DAY 275

"Who you spend time with is who you become.
Finding a positive peer group of people who challenge you and who are
smarter than you will help you become a real-life superhero."

~ Jim Kwik

DAY 276

*"If we used our body like we used our mind,
we'd only move our little finger."*

~ Bob Proctor

*"Never forget how powerful and truly magnificent
you are!"*

~ Bob Proctor

DAY 277

"It is the desire of God that you should get rich. He wants you to get rich because he can express himself better through you if you have plenty of things to use in giving him expression. He can live more in you if you have unlimited command of the means of life."

~ Wallace D. Wattles

DAY 278

*"I want you to lie to your mind,
cheat fear, and steal back the phenomenal
confidence you were born with."*

~ Marisa Peer

DAY 279

"Your perspective is always limited by how much you know. Expand your knowledge and you will transform your mind."

~ Bruce H. Lipton

DAY 280

"Peace is not absence of conflict, it is the ability to handle conflict by peaceful means."

~ Ronald Reagan

DAY 281

"Thoughts are real forces; the thoughts we think determine our attitude, actions and ultimately our outcomes. Raise the quality of your thoughts and success will follow."

~ Robin Banks

DAY 282

*"Even the darkest night will end and
the sun will rise."*

~ Victor Hugo

DAY 283

"Whatever we plant in our subconscious mind and nourish with repetition and emotion will one day become a reality."

~ Earl Nightingale

DAY 284

"The actor has to develop his body.
The actor has to work on his voice.
But the most important thing the actor has to work on is his mind."

~ Stella Adler

DAY 285

"Most people coast along safely in life until they die."

~ Bob Proctor

"True knowledge exists in knowing that you know nothing."

~ Socrates

DAY 286

"You can't connect the dots looking forward; you can only connect them looking backwards. So you have to trust that the dots will somehow connect in your future. You have to trust in something – your gut, destiny, life, karma, whatever. This approach has never let me down, and it has made all the difference in my life."

~ Steve Jobs

DAY 287

"Most people do not really want freedom, because freedom assumes responsibility and most people are afraid of that responsibility."

~ Sigmund Freud

DAY 288

"Change your thoughts and you change your world."

~ Norman Vincent Peale

DAY 289

"The weak can never forgive. Forgiveness is the attribute of the strong."

~ Mahatma Gandhi

DAY 290

*"If you want life to give you what you wish,
make sure you order what you want."*

~ Mirela Sula

DAY 291

"If somebody offers you an amazing opportunity but you are not sure you can do it, say yes – then learn how to do it later!"

~ Richard Branson

DAY 292

"If you're going to quit anything,
Quit being lazy, quit making
Excuses and quit waiting for the right time."

~ Debbie Siebers

DAY 293

*"People are always blaming their circumstances for what they are.
I don't believe in circumstances.
The people who get on in this world are the people who get up and look for
the circumstances they want, and if they can't find them, make them."*

~ George Bernard Shaw

DAY 294

*"The creation of a thousand
forests is in one acorn."*

~ Ralph Waldo Emerson

DAY 295

"The real test is not whether you avoid failure, because you won't. It's whether you let it harden or shame you into inaction, or whether you learn from it; whether you choose to persevere."

~ Barack Obama

DAY 296

"Fear and growth go hand in hand. When you courageously
face the thing you fear,
you automatically experience the growth
you have been seeking."

~ Sandy Gallagher

DAY 297

"The soul is placed in the body like a rough diamond, and must be polished, or the luster of it will never appear."

~ Daniel Defoe

"Take time to listen to your intuition."

~ Marie Diamond

DAY 298

"Complaining about your current position in life is worthless. Have a spine and do something about it instead."

~ Robert Kyosaki

DAY 299

"Be kind, for everyone you meet is fighting a hard battle."

~ Plato

"Courage is knowing what not to fear."

~ Plato

DAY 300

"Epic things start with small humble steps.
Pay respect to your beginnings. And if you're just starting out,
know that it's OK to be sucky.
To be small. To be messy and chaotic.
Just make sure to never ever stop dreaming."

~ Vishen Lakhiani

DAY 301

*"Gratitude places you in the energy field of plentitude.
Glow with gratitude and see how awe and joy
will make their home in you."*

~ Michael Beckwith

DAY 302

"When you can collaborate with your mind and tell it what you want, you will get what you want."

~ Marisa Peer

DAY 303

"The greatest astonishment of my life was the discovery that the man who does the work is not the man who gets rich."

~ Andrew Carnegie

DAY 304

"Let's start with what we can be thankful for, and get our mind into that vibration, and then watch the good that starts to come, because one thought leads to another thought."

~ Bob Proctor

DAY 305

*"If you never see great riches in your imagination,
you will never see them in your bank balance."*

~ Napoleon Hill

DAY 306

"Every man's happiness is his own responsibility."

~ Abraham Lincoln

"You are what you do, not what you say you'll do."

~ Carl Jung

DAY 307

*"NOW is the time. The Universe likes SPEED.
Don't delay, don't second-guess, don't doubt.
When the opportunity or impulse is there...ACT!"*

~ Joe Vitale

DAY 308

"True abundance has nothing to do with what I am having,
but everything to do with what I am being."

~ Neale Donald Walsch

DAY 309

"God's greatest gift to you is your unlimited potential. Your greatest gift to God is to use that potential to the fullest."

~ James Arthur Ray

"The only competition you will have is the competition between your disciplined and undisciplined mind."

~ James Arthur Ray

DAY 310

*"When you give yourself permission to have made mistakes in the past –
when you begin to trust yourself about making new choices – that's when
your intuition becomes reliable and trustworthy."*

~ Lisa Nichols

DAY 311

"Our environment, the world in which we live and work, is a mirror of our attitudes and expectations."

~ Earl Nightingale

"Your future is created by what you do today, not tomorrow."

~ Robert Kiyosaki

"Glorify who you are today, do not condemn who you were yesterday, and dream of who you can be tomorrow."

~ Neale Donald Walsch

"Tell the world what you intend to do, but, first, show it."

~ Napoleon Hill

DAY 312

*"You are the only problem you will ever have
and you are the only solution.
Change is inevitable,
personal growth is always a personal decision."*

~ Bob Proctor

DAY 313

"One looks back with appreciation to the brilliant teachers, but with gratitude to those who touched our human feelings.
The curriculum is so much necessary raw material, but warmth is the vital element for the growing plant and for the soul of the child."

~ Carl Jung

DAY 314

"You can convey the impression of increase by holding the unshakable faith that you are in the way of increase and by letting this faith inspire, fill, and permeate every action."

~ Wallace D. Wattles

DAY 315

"Affirmations repeated over and over again with feeling will create the belief system required in order to experience the results."

~ Peggy McColl

DAY 316

"Find what you love and be brilliant at it."

~ Marisa Peer

DAY 317

"He who lives in the realization of his oneness with this Infinite Power becomes a magnet to attract to himself a continual supply of whatsoever things he desires.
The one who is truly wise, and who uses the forces and powers with which they are endowed, to them the great universe always opens her treasure house."

~ Ralph Waldo Trine

DAY 318

"Happy people build their inner world;
unhappy people blame their outer world."

~ Dalai Lama

DAY 319

"The moment you change your perception, is
the moment you rewrite the chemistry of your body."

~ Bruce H. Lipton

DAY 320

"The size of your success is measured
by the strength of your desire;
the size of your dream; and how you
handle disappointment along the way."

~ Robert Kiyosaki

DAY 321

"You can't push anyone up the ladder unless
he is willing to climb himself."

~ Andrew Carnegie

DAY 322

"Do your work; not just your work and no more but a little more for the lavishing's sake, that little more which is worth all the rest, and if you suffer as you must then you doubt as you must, do your work, and the sky will clear and then out of your very doubt and suffering will be born the supreme joy of life."

~ Dean Briggs

DAY 323

"The moment you realize you already have everything
You're looking for, the universe gives it to you."

~ John Frederick Demartini

DAY 324

"All people are who they are because of their dominating thoughts and desires."

~ Napoleon Hill

DAY 325

"Whoever is happy will make others happy too."

~ Anne Frank

"You make your beliefs and then your beliefs make you."

~ Marisa Peer

DAY 326

"Man is buffeted by circumstances so long as he believes himself to be the creature of outside conditions.
But when he realizes that he is a creative power, and that he may command the hidden soil and seeds of his being out of which circumstances grow, he then becomes the rightful master of himself."

~ James Allen

DAY 327

"It's not the lack of resources, it's your lack of resourcefulness that stops you."

~ Tony Robbins

DAY 328

"Mind is the greatest power in all of creation."

~ J.B.Rhine

*"Humanity is acquiring all the right technology
for all the wrong reasons."*

~ R. Buckminster Fuller

DAY 329

"And above all, watch with glittering eyes the whole world around you because the greatest secrets are always hidden in the most unlikely places. Those who don't believe in magic will never find it."

~ Roald Dahl

DAY 330

"We all possess more power and greater possibilities than we realize, and visualizing is one of the greatest of these powers."

~ Genevieve Behrend

DAY 331

"Most people are not going after what they want.
Even some of the most serious goal seekers and goal setters,
they're going after what they think they can get."

~ Bob Proctor

DAY 332

"It is curious that physical courage should be so common in the world and moral courage so rare."

~ Mark Twain

DAY 333

"Quality means doing it right when no one is looking."

~ Henry Ford

DAY 334

"In learning you will teach, and in teaching you will learn."

~ Phil Collins

DAY 335

"Decide what you want. Believe you can have it. Believe you deserve it and believe it's possible for you. And then close your eyes and every day for several minutes, visualize having what you already want, feeling the feelings of already having it.
Come out of that and focus on what you're grateful for already, and really enjoy it. Then go into your day and release it to the Universe and trust that the Universe will figure out how to manifest it."

~ Jack Canfield

DAY 336

"Please quit overthinking everything.
Stop obsessing over your failures.
Stop doubting yourself and seeing greatness in everyone else but you.
You are better than that. You deserve more.
Start showing up differently."

~ Lewis Howes

DAY 337

"We fail to achieve success because we do not try to understand ourselves better. We do not try and connect to spirit; to be serene. Instead we catch a glint of gold, try and dig here and there, following the glittered surface we spot, instead of focusing to dig the gold from our own garden."

~ Vladimira Kuna

DAY 338

*"I claim not to have controlled events but confess plainly
that events have controlled me."*

~ Abraham Lincoln

"Time is an illusion."

~ Albert Einstein

DAY 339

"All you need is the plan, the road map, and the courage to press on to your destination."

~ Earl Nightingale

DAY 340

"Let us not look back in anger, nor forward in fear,
but around us in awareness."

~ Leland Val Van De Wall

DAY 341

"There are two primary choices in life:
To accept conditions as they exist or accept the responsibility
for changing them."

~ Denis Waitley

DAY 342

"At some point you have to own up to how great you are, how beautiful you are, to how much inner dignity and potential you have.
Drop complaining about what other people didn't give you or do for you, or how they mistreated you.
Take repossession of your Self and you will rise to a level of greatness that has been yours all along."

~ Michael Beckwith

DAY 343

"Do you want to know what you think about most of the time? Take a look at the results you're getting. That will tell you exactly What's going on inside."

~ Bob Proctor

"If you do not get the chills when you set your goal you're not setting big enough goals."

~ Bob Proctor

"See yourself living in abundance and you will attract it. It always works, it works every time with every person."

~ Bob Proctor

DAY 344

"Explore and tap into your gifts, there is always more potential inside you."

~ Mirela Sula

"Remember, your mind is your greatest asset, so be careful what you put into it."

~ Robert Kiyosaki

DAY 345

"Self-creation never ends. You are continually creating yourself from the field of infinite possibilities. You are, in every moment, born again. And so is everyone else."

~ Neale Donald Walsch

DAY 346

"People who are very successful never ever wait for motivation. They do it because when you do it you become motivated."

~ Marisa Peer

DAY 347

"Everything you seek and everything you experience – everything – is inside you. If you want to change anything, you do it inside, not outside. The whole idea is total responsibility. There's no one to blame. It's all you."

~ Joe Vitale

DAY 348

*"If we wait for anything outside of us to make us happy,
then we are not following the quantum law.
We are relying on the outer to change the inner."*

~ Dr. Joe Dispenza

DAY 349

*"God has strewn our paths with wonders
and we certainly should not go through life
with our eyes shut."*

~ Alexander Graham Bell

DAY 350

*"If you are not consciously directing your life,
you will lose your footing and circumstances
will decide for you."*

~ Michael Beckwith

"The pain pushes you, until the vision pulls you."

~ Michael Beckwith

DAY 351

"You are an energetic being.
You are expressing energy and attracting energy.
And, quite simply you attract based on how you feel."

~ Peggy McColl

DAY 352

"Happiness cannot be traveled to, owned, earned, worn or consumed. Happiness is the spiritual experience of living every minute with love, grace and gratitude."

~ Denis Waitley

DAY 353

"And while the law of competition may be sometimes hard for the individual, it is best for the race because it ensures the survival of the fittest in every department."

~ Andrew Carnegie

DAY 354

*"Have you ever fully realized that life is,
after all, merely a series of habits, and that it lies entirely
within one's own power to determine
just what that series shall be?"*

~ Ralph Waldo Trine

DAY 355

"Faith is the 'eternal elixir' which gives life, power and action to the impulse of thought!"

~ Napoleon Hill

DAY 356

> *"So many of us are leading limited lives not because we have to but because we THINK we have to."*
>
> **~ Bruce H. Lipton**

DAY 357

*"Earth provides enough to satisfy every man's needs,
but not every man's greed."*

~ **Mahatma Gandhi**

*"You are the designer of your destiny;
you are the author of your story."*

~ **Lisa Nichols**

DAY 358

"The meeting of two personalities
vis like the contact of two chemical substances:
If there is any reaction, both are transformed."

~ Carl Jung

DAY 359

"Persistence is probably the single most common quality of high achievers. They simply refuse to give up. The longer you hang in there, the greater the chance that something will happen in your favor. No matter how hard it seems, the longer you persist the more likely your success."

~ Jack Canfield

DAY 360

"You're never defeated until you accept something as defeat."

~ Helen Keller

DAY 361

"The imagination will take you where no one has gone.
You can see what has never yet materialized.
It deals with the 'might be' element of life."

~ Sandy Gallagher

DAY 362

"People who succeed
Do what they need to do first,
To get where they want to be."

~ Marisa Peer

DAY 363

"As I grow older, I pay less attention to what men say. I just watch what they do."

~ Andrew Carnegie

"Problems can only exist If they have your attention."

~ Michael Beckwith

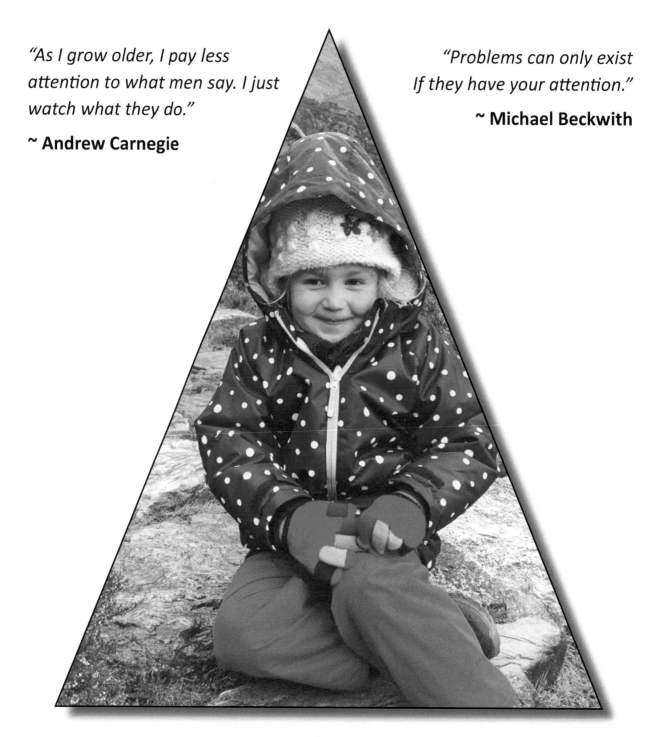

DAY 364

"Behind every problem,
there is a question trying to ask itself.

Behind every question, there's an answer
trying to reveal itself.

Behind every answer, there's an action
trying to take place.

And behind every action,
there's a way of life trying to be born."

~ **Michael Beckwith**

DAY 365

"A mentor is someone who sees
more talent and ability within you,
than you see in yourself,
and helps bring it out of you."

~ Bob Proctor

Day 231 – Carl Jung
Day 228 – Peggy McColl
Day 183 – Peggy McColl
Day 40 – Jesus
Day 53 – Socrates
Day 136 – Bear Gryllis
Day 147 – Mother Theresa
Day 263 – Mother Theresa
Day 351 – Peggy McColl

My "To Be" List:

1. Be enough and worthy.
2. BE aware and have a phenomenal attitude.
3. BE lovable and kind.
4. BE grateful and faithful.
5. BE open-minded and make decisions fast.
6. BE responsible and take action.
7. BE confident and creative.
8. BE persistent and organized.
9. BE abundant and serene.
10. BE ME and trust my powerful mind and emotions.

Vladimira Kuna

About The Author

Vladimirakuna.com
facebook.com/vladikuna
Instagram: vladimirakuna_author

Vladimira Kuna is Slovak-born author, who lives in Harpenden, UK. She has two children, a son and daughter who have unleashed her hidden power of writing. She loves books and Personal Development studies. Vladimira is a passionate student of Bob Proctor, a mentor and the master thinker. When it comes to systematizing life, no one else can touch him. He is simply the best.

She is also mentored by the amazing Peggy McColl, a world-renowned wealth, business and manifestation expert as well as a New York Times best-selling Author. Peggy is a master at manifesting and helped her to change her results and her life.

Recommended Books That Have Influenced Me:

- *The Bible*
- *You Were Born Rich* by Bob Proctor
- *Think and Grow Rich* by Napoleon Hill
- *Your Invisible Power* by Genevieve Behrend
- *The Secret* by Rhonda Byrne
- *The Power* by Rhonda Byrne
- *As a Man Thinketh* by James Allen
- *Chicken Soup for the Soul* by Jack Canfield & Mark Victor Hansen
- *The Demand Principle* by Peggy McColl
- *The Science of Getting Rich* by Wallace D. Wattles
- *Seven Lost Secrets of Success* by Joe Vitale
- *The Four Agreements* by Don Miguel Ruiz
- *The Memory Book* by Harry Lorayne & Jerry Lucas
- *The Power of Your Subconscious Mind* by Joseph Murphy
- *The Book of the Shepherd* by Joann Davis
- *The Alchemist* by Paulo Coelho
- *Edinburgh Lectures on Mental Science* by Thomas Troward
- *The Power of Awareness* by Neville Goddard

How To Use This Book Effectively?

I suggest you choose
three powerful statements
that resonate with your heart
and read them
all day long for 30 days!

I am passionate about helping others, therefore I am happy and grateful that
I can help others by donating a portion of the net proceeds from this book to the following:

HSoA (Harpenden Spotlight on Africa) under registration number 1117585;
www.hsoa.org.uk
Support our orphans and vulnerable children programme.

*   *   *

Orbis UK (Orbis Charitable Trust),
under registration number 1061352,
company number 3303689
gbr.orbis.org
Give the gift of Sight

HEARTS to be HEARD

Giving a Voice to Creativity!

With every donation, a voice will be given to
the creativity that lies within the hearts of
our children living with diverse challenges.

By making this difference, children that may
not have been given the opportunity to have their
Heart Heard will have the freedom to create
beautiful works of art and musical creations.

Donate by visiting
HeartstobeHeard.com

We thank you.